ACCUSED

I, WITNESS

ACCUSED

My Story of Injustice

Adama Bah

Norton Young Readers

An Imprint of W. W. Norton & Company
Independent Publishers Since 1923

To my parents, Mamadou and Aissatou, and to my siblings, Alpha, Maraima, Abdoul, and Saeed.

CONTENTS

INTRODUCTION

Zainab Nasrati, Zoë Ruiz, and Dave Eggers

One of the best ways to understand a complicated issue is through the story of a person who lived at the center of it. If you want to learn about what would drive a sixteen-year-old to fight for young women's rights to education in Burundi, why not hear from that person directly? This is what this series is all about: letting young people—who have seen and lived through recent history—tell their stories.

It's important to understand other people's struggles, especially people who live in different places or come from different backgrounds than you do. Our hope with this book series is that by hearing one person's story, our readers will learn about many people's struggles and think about what we can do together to help make the world better.

Teenagers like Malala Yousafzai and Greta Thunberg became iconic for standing up for what they believe is right. Other teens, not yet as well known, have also stepped up to make a difference. When Salvador Gómez-Colón was a teenager, Hurricane Maria hit his hometown of San Juan, Puerto Rico, and he jumped into action, helping people in need there. When Gilda Temaj was only sixteen, she had to leave her home in Guatemala alone and make her way to the United States. Now that she's a college student, Gilda is studying to become a lawyer so she can help others who seek safe haven in the United States.

The I, Witness books will bring you stories of ordinary kids and teens like you who have faced extraordinary challenges in their lives. Their stories are exciting and surprising. At times they are sad, and at others they are joyful. We hope that you will consider your own life and your own story as you read. Is your life very similar to the author's? Or very different? Is there a problem in the world or in your life that you would like to help solve?

In this book, you'll meet Adama Bah, who was arrested and put in jail as a young teenager because she was wrongly accused of crimes. While it's unlikely that many of our readers will face such an awful circumstance, we know that many of us will be misjudged by our appearance like Adama was or we will face a different terrifying, unexpected situation. As readers ourselves, we learned so much from the way Adama persevered through these difficulties. We hope that you will be encouraged and strengthened by her story, as we are.

ACCUSED

CHAPTER 1

Unsheltered

I didn't know I wasn't an American until I was sixteen and I was in handcuffs.

I was born in Conakry, the capital city of Guinea, in 1988. In Africa and in many developing countries, people hear about the riches to be had in America. It's the land of opportunity. My dad left behind his life of farming in Guinea and came to America for the promise of a new life. He settled in Brooklyn, working as a cabdriver and saving money to bring our family over to the United States. The year I turned two, I came to the United States with my mother and we joined my father in New York. After my mother and I moved to America, my four younger siblings—three brothers and one sister— were born in the United States.

While growing up in New York, I always had many "cousins" around. They were all Guinean immigrants. They weren't my real family, but they were my neighbors and our closeness bonded us like blood. We created a community together thousands of miles away from the country that bred us. The friends that I had in New York were Latinx and African American. During my youth, I fit in with them. We all experienced the same issues, like boys, gossip, and puberty. I wish those were the problems that I thought about now.

I went to public school until the seventh grade. At that point, my dad decided that I should learn about my religion, so he sent me to an Islamic boarding school in Buffalo, New York. Looking back, my family was never really that religious, but my dad had heard about the school from somebody who recommended it and he decided to send me there.

I was thirteen years old on September 11, 2001. That day, all of the teachers came in late and had the students sit in a huge circle. My teacher said, "I have to talk to you guys. For those of you who are from New York City, I want you to brace yourselves. I have some bad news. Sometimes things happen in life that we don't understand." She started talking about God and how to be patient and steadfast. Then she said, "The Twin Towers were hit today."

I freaked out. I panicked and tried desperately to reach my family, but I couldn't get in contact with them. When my teacher called us back for a second meeting, she announced that a Muslim might have been behind the attack and that it might cause public hatred toward the Islamic community.

"What do you mean?" I asked. "They think we all did it? We didn't plot it. I don't have nothing to do with it. Why would we all be blamed for it?" So many thoughts raced through my head: Who is Osama bin Laden? Why would he do this? This act is against Islam. None of us at the school knew who bin Laden was. The other students and I started to make jokes about him. My friends said to me, "Your name is very close to his name: Adama, Osama." We laughed.

The next day, someone threw a rock through the window of the school. I couldn't understand what would motivate someone to do that—the boarding school was an education center, a place for learning and safety. We weren't plotting anything, and we certainly didn't support Osama bin Laden. A couple of weeks later, I was finally able to talk to my family and they told me that they were fine. My dad said, "Shh, don't even talk about it. Be quiet. Goodbye." He refused to discuss anything over the phone, afraid that someone was listening.

I felt the effect of 9/11 in the tense air when I went back to New York two months later for Ramadan break. There were six of us students who had to get on a plane to go back to the city. We wore clothing that I had started to wear when I went to boarding school. The clothing was pitch-black and covered our faces and bodies. We were even wearing gloves; all you could see were our eyes, peering out of black fabric figures. I couldn't believe the way people stared at us. They pointed at us and turned red, hurrying away from us in the airport. Whispers of, "What's going on?" flitted among my classmates. We were terrified. I thought that those strangers were going to attack me in public. At boarding school, we had been sheltered. We didn't know what was going on around the country. We didn't know about the hate crimes—we didn't know anything. We hadn't expected to be treated like this.

That day at the airport, the six of us were

given extra screenings compared to the other passengers. Our bags were checked with careful eyes and we were pulled to the side for more inspection. We were marked as suspicious based on our clothing and our religion. The security guards were nasty to us; the passengers were nasty to us; the airline workers were nasty to us. When my classmates and I boarded the plane, the pilot took one look at us and shook his head. It made me feel awful. Strangers cursed at us, yelled at us, and sucked their teeth, saying, "Go back to your country, you Talibani! Go back to Osama bin Laden!"

I was being singled out for a crime I didn't commit. I was being judged as guilty without any trial at all. I was thirteen and I had never experienced anything like this. I had never been the subject of discrimination based on my race or religion; I had always been sheltered from horrible things like that, surrounded by members of my community who understood and related to me. For my whole life I had felt untouchable because I was American. On that plane, I felt terrible. I couldn't believe the inhumanity that was being directed toward me. I had no idea that this was far from the worst treatment I would receive for my identity in America.

CHAPTER 2

Taken

My parents didn't know that I wore Islamic garb until I came home. When my mom opened the door and saw me dressed entirely in black, she let go of the door. I walked into the apartment and she said to my father, "You have to tell her to take this off. I told you not to send her to that school!"

They disapproved of my niqab, the traditional garment I wore, which covered everything but my eyes. They urged me to take it off, worried for my safety in this new, post-9/11 world.

When I had originally left for school, New York City was peaceful and happy. People would smile and say hello to me when I walked down the street. But when I came back after 9/11, I was greeted with hostility. The city's air was filled with fear. People didn't take the time to talk to me or ask me why I was wearing a niqab. When I walked down the street, people would curse at me and even throw things. Their mean reactions actually made me want to wear it more because I thought my faith was being tested. I didn't want to be pulled away from my faith. I wanted to be strong.

My parents removed me from the boarding school in Buffalo and I went back to public school for the ninth grade. Every day I dressed in my niqab, even though I was the only one at my school who wore one. I started wearing colored contacts when the other girls started wearing makeup. I thought that I might as well make something look pretty; if people couldn't see my face, they could look at my nice eyes! It was a way of feeling beautiful in clothes that concealed me. Despite the way the general public treated me, I didn't have many problems in high school. The only thing the other kids always bothered me about was asking to see my face. My classmates would tease me about my hidden appearance, saying, "I wonder how you look under there. You're probably ugly." We would make jokes about it. I'd say, "Yeah, I look hideous. That's why I always wear it, of course!" But after a few months of attending public school, I thought, *This is not a mosque. This is not my old Islamic boarding school.* So, in the middle of the ninth grade, I took off my niqab. I walked into school still wearing an abaya, which is a long, loose robe, but with my face uncovered. My teacher just looked at me, surprised, and said, "Adama?" I remember all of the students coming into the room just to look at me in the middle of English class, to see what

I looked like. They were nice to me. They said things like, "Oh, you're not ugly! You have nice teeth."

"Thank you," I replied, smiling for all of them to see.

The morning of March 24, 2005, my mother, my siblings, and I were in our apartment sleeping when a pounding at the door woke us up. My mom got up and went to open it. Suddenly a group of people barged in, disturbing the peace in our home. I had been sleeping with a blanket over my head and someone ripped it off of me. I froze and looked up at the man standing over me. "You've got to get up!" he said. I didn't understand what was going on. The man forced me out of bed and made me sit in the living room with my family. I saw about ten or fifteen people spilling out of our apartment into the hallway. They were mostly men, but there were also two women. Some had FBI jackets, and others were from the police department and the Department of Homeland Security. They went through papers, threw our stuff around, shouted, talked to each other. They were like a destructive storm in our apartment. I heard them yelling at my mother, who didn't speak much English. They pulled her into the kitchen, screaming, "We're going to deport you and your whole family!"

I was in shock and my thoughts were swirling in my head. What's going on? What are they talking about? I knew my dad had an issue with his immigration papers, but I didn't think that my mom did. They kept saying, "We're going to send all of you back to your country."

Then my dad walked into the apartment in handcuffs. They had gone to the mosque to detain him. It was the scariest thing I had ever seen: my father standing there powerless. He was always the strong one, the guy no one messed with. He was not someone you argued with. If he said do it, you did it. And here he was, handcuffed and helpless for both himself and his family. They took him to the kitchen and whispered something to him. He sat down, looked at us, and said,

"Everything's going to be fine. Don't worry." But I knew that nothing was fine. I knew that something was horribly wrong.

The men told my dad to tell us what was going on. He said that they were going to arrest him and take him away. Then the FBI agents told me to get up and get my shoes. I thought they wanted to see my sneaker collection— I had all types of sneakers in different colors. I grabbed them and brought them to the agents. Showing them off, I said, "I have this one, I have this one, I have this one."

One of the agents said, "Choose one."

My favorite color is blue, so I picked up a blue pair and told the agent, "This one."

He said, "Put them on."

I said, "Okay, but I know they fit me."

"Put them on!" He was very nasty. Then he said, "All those earrings have to go." I have eight piercings in each ear, a nose ring, and a tongue ring. I went to the kitchen to take them all out and the men followed me. I could taste the sourness of my breath, so I asked, "Can I at least brush my teeth? My breath stinks really bad. Can I use the bathroom?"

"No. We have to go. You're coming with us," they said.

"Where am I going? Am I going with my dad?" I put on my jacket, and they let me put on my headscarf and abaya. Then one of the women took out handcuffs. I felt dread sink into me and I started to panic. "What did I do? Where are we going?" I asked, stuttering as she locked them around my wrists. I was sixteen years old and I was in handcuffs. I looked to my dad for guidance, and he said, "Just do what they say."

My mom didn't know I was being taken. When we got out the door, she said in broken English, "Where she go? Where she go?"

The agents said, "We're taking her." The man who seemed to be in charge put his hands on my mother to hold her back. When the door slammed shut, neither of us knew when we would see each other again.

CHAPTER 3

Questioned

The agents took my dad and me outside and put us in an Escalade. I was terrified. I asked my father, "What's going on? What's going to happen?" He said, "Don't say anything. We're going to get a lawyer. It's okay. Everything is going to be fine." I paid attention to my surroundings. Two Escalades drove along with us. I looked around, trying to map out my landscape. I recognized the Brooklyn Bridge and many other landmarks, but I didn't recognize the building my father and I were taken to. We got out of the car and walked past a security booth before taking a ramp beneath the building to the parking lot. Once we were inside the building, they separated me from my father and put me in a white cell with a bench. There were no bars or windows, but there was a door that had a tiny glass pane that I could look through. I could see a bunch of computers and tables and people walking back and forth and talking. I could see other cell doors. When they opened one of those doors, I could see my dad inside, and they were talking to him. I don't know how long I was in my cell. I was nervous, I was panicking, I was crying, I was trying to figure out what was going on, and I was constantly using the bathroom. The toilet was open to the rest of the cell. There was a camera on the ceiling in the middle of the room and I wondered if they were watching me pee. There were blankets in the cell, and I wrapped them around myself to use the toilet.

Some time later, I was taken out of my cell to be interrogated. It was just me and a man sitting among the computers. There was a guy all the way down at the other end of the hall with my dad, but that was it. Throughout this whole experience, no one had told me who they were. The man I sat with asked me questions like, "What's your name? What's your age? What's your date of birth? Where were you born?" He already knew the answers to all of these questions. He knew that I was born in Guinea. Then he asked, "What is your citizenship status?" I said, "American." He kept asking me about my citizenship status. Then after a while he said, "You know you're not here legally, right? You know why you're here today, right? You weren't born in this country. Do you know that you're not an American?"

For a second I felt rage toward my parents. It was as if one of the biggest secrets in the world had just been revealed to me and I was at its center. I don't know if my parents concealed my status from me to protect them or to protect me, but either way, being told the truth was shocking. The man's attitude didn't change when he realized I had no idea what was going on. He continued to be mean to me. He sat there explaining what was going to happen to me. He asked me if I wanted to see a consular officer.

I asked, "What is a consular officer?"

He said, "You don't know what a consular

officer is? Those are people from your country. From Guinea."

I said, "What about them? What do I have to see them for?"

Finally, they called my dad. They gave us a document about how we could see a consular officer. My dad knows how to read English, but he said to me in Pular, a language widely spoken in Guinea, "Pretend you're translating to me in my language." Then he said, "Whatever you do, do not say you can go back to your country. They will circumcise you there."

My dad wasn't just coming up with an excuse to stay. There was a real fear of female genital mutilation in Guinea. It happened to my mom. In order to get married in Guinea, a female would have to be circumcised. It isn't required by law, but instead by culture. My dad's brothers would do it; they would make sure I got circumcised. My parents made a decision when they had daughters that they would never let that happen to us. That's the main reason why our parents never took us back to Guinea, not even to visit.

The interrogation agent told my dad, "Hey, you've got to get up, you've got to leave." To me they said, "We have to fingerprint you." When we were done with the fingerprints, they took a picture of me. I was then sitting on a bench in the main entrance when a young lady I recognized walked in. Her name was Tashnuba. I had seen her at the mosque before, but I didn't know her personally. I said hello to her, but in my heart, I was panicking. What is she doing here? Who am I going to see next? Finally, I was brought to another room that had a table with three chairs at it, one on one side and two opposite it. A federal agent walked in and said to me, "I need to talk to you about something." The questions she started asking had nothing to do with immigration. They were questions about terrorism. She asked me about locations and people. She went down a list of people and asked if I knew them. I didn't know who they were. She mentioned people from London and from all over the world. As time went on, different officials started asking me questions at different times. There was the CIA, the FBI, and NYPD. I thought, What's going on? I am not the person that you think I am! My situation was even worse than I had originally believed.

CHAPTER 4

Framed

A male interrogator told me that the religious study group Tashnuba was part of had been started by a guy who was wanted by the FBI. I had no idea if this was true or not. The study group at the mosque was all women. It was a resource for women learning about religion, women's empowerment, why we cover ourselves, how we pray, when to pray—things like that. There was nothing about jihad or anything violent. It was mostly for converts and new people who had just come into Islam. I wasn't a part of the group, but the agents asked me about it and told me they'd taken my computer and my diary. My diary was a black-and-white notebook that I wrote everything down in. I had phone numbers, I had notes, I had stories in it; I had everything. They asked me about every contact in there, about every little thing I had written. But there was nothing in there about jihad. There was nothing in there about anything illegal. There was nothing suspicious in the notebook at all, so I wasn't worried.

They said, "We have your computer. We can find whatever you're hiding."

"Go ahead, look in my computer. I have nothing to hide," I replied.

They kept making a scene, like there was something big I was hiding. They said, "Don't lie to us. If you lie to us, we'll have proof. We'll catch you in your lie." Although I knew there was nothing in my computer, all of their intense questioning made me start to doubt myself. I thought, Okay, what's going on now? Is there something bad in there? Their technique was to make me question what I knew, and it was working. But then I thought, Wait a minute—I'm not this person they say. What are they talking about?

The interrogation lasted a long time. A Secret Service agent came in and asked me how I felt about President Bush. I said, "I don't like him," but they didn't seem to care. I was being very honest with them. There was nothing to hide. The Secret Service guy was aggressive. He said, "I don't understand— why do you choose to cover when women choose to wear less and less every day?"

I said, "It's freedom of choice. Some people want to show some stuff, some people want to hide some things. Some people want to preserve their bodies, and some people don't want to. Some people want to show it to the whole world."

He said, "I don't understand. You're

young. Why are you doing this?" Then the agents asked me about Tashnuba. They asked me about her name and her family, but I told them that I didn't know her. They said, "Tashnuba wrote you on this list."

"What list?" I asked.

"She signed you up to be a suicide bomber."

"Are you serious? Why would she do that? She doesn't seem like that type of person," I said. They were trying to make it seem like I was wrong about who I knew and who I didn't know.

They allowed me to leave the interrogation room briefly because my dad wanted to talk to me. They had him sign papers consenting to let them talk to me because I was underage. We didn't know that we were supposed to have lawyers. The FBI never told us that.

My dad said, "Everything is going to be fine. I want you to be brave. I'll see you later."

Back in the interrogation room, the agents told me that Tashnuba and I were going to leave. "Where's my dad? Can I say 'bye to him?" I asked. They told me that he had already left. I started to cry; I'd had my dad there the whole time, and without him I felt alone and even more afraid. "Where is he going to go? What are you guys going to do?" They said that he was going to see an immigration judge before the day ended.

I asked, "When am I going to see him?

Where am I going?" They told me to stop with the questions. They brought in Tashnuba and handcuffed us both with our hands behind our backs. The cuffs were tight and uncomfortable, and they left marks on my wrists. We were led outside. Again, I paid attention to my surroundings. We were put back into an Escalade. I tried to take note of landmarks we passed along the way. I didn't recognize where they took us, but it was on Varick Street in Manhattan. When we arrived at our destination, the agent told us to walk in casually among all of the people passing on the street. He said, "Act casual and people won't say anything."

Once we were inside, Tashnuba and

I were put into an elevator alone. We went up and entered a large room that was divided into smaller holding cells, which didn't have bars but were enclosed with glass. The two of us were put into our own cell. From there, we saw a bunch of men in orange jumpsuits in one of the other cells yelling and screaming and we didn't know why. Agents had us turn our backs, and Tashnuba and I just looked at each other.

She said to me, "You put me on a list?"

I said, "No! They said you put me on a list."

We both realized that they had been trying to set us up. They didn't have anything on us at all, and I never found out why I was reported as a suicide bomber. They had come for Tashnuba early in the morning, too. They hadn't detained her parents, only her. Later, I found out why they'd taken my dad: After I'd been reported as a suicide bomber, the FBI started investigating my entire family. That's how they found out about my dad being in the United States without proper documentation.

Tashnuba and I tried to figure out what was going on, what they were going to do, if they were going to release us. That's when an officer walked into our cell. She said, "What are you guys in for?"

We said, "We don't know."

"I hear you guys did something."

"What did we do?"

She ignored the question and said, "We're going to take you to Pennsylvania."

Tashnuba and I looked at each other. Pennsylvania? "What are we going to do in Pennsylvania?" I asked.

She answered, "They didn't tell you? There's a detention center there."

CHAPTER 5

Violated

The FBI drove us to Pennsylvania, across state lines, without my parents' permission. We arrived at the juvenile detention center late at night. When the agents dropped us off, I wanted to scream, *Please don't leave us!* I didn't want to be left there. I didn't know where I was. I had seen so many new faces and the thought of dealing with even more people was too much, but there was nothing I could do about it. A female guard told Tashnuba and me that we had to get strip-searched. We said that was against our religion.

The guard said, "It's either that or we hold you down."

"Hold me down and do what? I'm not doing a strip search," I said. I was stubborn, but I was in a situation where I had no choice.

So she said, "Who wants to go first?"

Tashnuba went first. They searched her hair, checked her body parts—they checked everything. She had to take a shower and change into the uniform they gave her and then she was taken somewhere else. After she went downstairs, the guard said, "Okay, your turn. You're going to have to take everything off. Take off whatever you feel comfortable with first."

I said, "I can't do this. I can't." I was in tears. My own mother doesn't look at me naked. That's my privacy. I said, "It must be against some law for you to do this to me."

She said, "No, it's not. You no longer have rights."

"Why not? What did I do?"

"You're just going to have to take your clothes off." I was crying, but she just looked at me and said, "Kids here sneak things in. I have to search you."

I had on my abaya, and that was the first thing I took off. The second thing I took off was my headscarf. Then I took off my top. Then my bra. I stopped there for a long moment. I put my hands across my chest in an attempt to preserve a little bit of dignity for myself.

She said, "Come on, I don't have all day."

I said, "I can't do this, I can't, I can't."

"Drop your pants." So I took off my pants, I took off my underwear, and I kept my legs closed against each other, trying to cover myself. I held myself together as much as I could. She said, "You cannot do that. You have to let loose or I'll call another guard and we'll hold you down and search you. This is your last warning. If you want me to call someone in, I'll call them in right now, but it's not going to be nice."

I said, "Okay." I let go of my arms.

She said, "Lift your breasts." I lifted my breasts. "Open your legs more." I opened my legs.

"Put your hands in there, to see there's nothing."

"There's nothing there!" I replied.

She said, "Just do it." I did it.

"Turn around, put your hands up." I did that.

"All right, now put your fingers in your hair, pull at your ears. Show me your ears, open your mouth." I showed my mouth.

She said, "Show me up your nose," and I did.

Then she gave me a blue uniform: sweatpants, socks, underwear, a bra, and a hair tie, plus a little towel and a washcloth. She told me I had five minutes to take a shower and then she left. I knew I only had a short time, but I just sat at the corner of the shower and held myself and cried. I couldn't believe what I had just gone through. I was crying and crying and crying—it was all I could do. I don't know how long I sat there, but finally I told myself that I had to get up. I washed myself quickly.

I've never felt like I needed God more than I did on this day. So, I did *ghusl*, which is like a special shower before prayer. I prayed, "God, you've got to hear me for this one. I've never asked for anything that I desperately needed before." I dried myself with the small towel and put my uniform on. There was a little mirror in the room and I looked into it. My eyes were red from crying. The guard returned and told me I had to take off my headscarf. I said, "It's part of my religion." She let me keep the scarf, but later the supervisor took it from me.

I was taken to a cell. As we walked, the guard said, "You must keep your hands to your sides at all times." I was told to look straight ahead; I wasn't allowed to look anywhere else. There were cameras everywhere, but I wasn't listening to the rule. I was looking around. I still had no idea why I was here. I didn't know if it was an immigration issue or if it had to do with the things they had interrogated me about. When I got to the cell, all of the lights were out. I could see Tashnuba in the corner, praying.

There was only one blanket and it was freezing cold in the cell. We stayed up the whole night talking. I found out her mom had just had a baby; my mom had just had a baby, too. Tashnuba was the oldest sibling; I was the oldest. We were the same age. I asked what school she went to, what she was studying, what she wanted to do with her life. We were normal teenage girls and we couldn't wrap our heads around why this was happening to us. We were laughing, like, "Pinch me. This is a prank."

She said, "Maybe it will be all be straightened out by tomorrow."

I'm not sure how we fell asleep, but at one point we were both crying.

CHAPTER 6

Bargained

I tried to contain my anger, but it was impossible. I was filled with rage—at the way I was being treated, at the FBI agents and the detention center guards, at America as a country. On my first morning in detention, we went for breakfast and were supposed to salute the American flag. I refused. "I'm not saluting it," I said. During the pledge I put my hands to my sides and stared out the window. Each morning I did that. One of the guards eventually asked me, "How come you don't pledge allegiance?"

"You guys said it yourself. I am not American."

For the first three weeks that I was there, my family didn't have any idea where I was. They had to do research to figure out my location and they hired a lawyer. Two lawyers came to see me at the detention center.

Natasha, one of the lawyers, asked me, "Do you know why you're here?" I said that I didn't.

"There's a rumor going around about you being a suicide bomber," the other lawyer said. I laughed so hard.

"That's not funny," he said. "Don't laugh."

"Are you serious or are you joking? If you knew me, you would laugh and say, *Hell, no*," I said. I had a family, an identity; I wanted to be alive. "I'm not ready to meet God yet."

"But they're not charging you with anything except overstaying your visa," Natasha said.

My mom came to visit me after my lawyer left. She was so skinny. I could tell she wasn't eating. It should have been good to see her, but her visit was awful because she didn't seem to want to talk at all. When I asked about my dad, she just said, "He's fine." It was clear that she was upset. She was so drained.

Nobody at the detention center would talk to me about what was going on. I wasn't brought before a judge until my fourth week there, and it was via video conference. An article came out in the *New York Times* about why Tashnuba and I were there, that we were suspected of being suicide bombers. After the guards read why we were being detained, things got worse. They would whisper, "There go those girls," or "There goes a terrorist."

After the article came out, we got extra strip searches, about three times a day, and the searches got stricter. They would tell us to spread our butt cheeks and they made awful, racist comments. The guards would laugh and say, "Look at those jerks. Look at them. These are the ones that want to take our country down." If I talked back, they told me that they would tackle me down and throw me into solitary confinement. All I wanted was to leave. I knew that I had to deal with whatever the guards said to me to avoid being sent to solitary.

Tashnuba and I also lost a lot of privileges because of our headscarves. We weren't allowed to use the bathroom privately. So, when I had to go to the bathroom with a guard, I thought, I hope I stink this place up. I pray that my poop will make this place close down. I hope my poop brings toxins. I tried everything, but nothing stopped the searches.

After a while, my lawyer called and told me she had good news. "I have a way to get you out of jail. You have to agree to wear an ankle bracelet, adhere to a curfew, and sign a gag order."

I said, "I'll wear anything."

The day that I was finally supposed to be released from the detention center, I said goodbye to Tashnuba in the cafeteria. I wanted to hold her and let her know everything was going to be okay, but I couldn't hug her or she would have been sent to solitary confinement. I just looked at her and said, "May Allah be with you, and be patient." Then I walked away. I haven't spoken to Tashnuba at all since then. She told me while we were both in the detention center that her mother made an agreement with the federal government: if they released her daughter, they would go back to their country, which I think was Bangladesh. Tashnuba was released about a week after me and she went straight to the airport.

I was at that detention center for six and a half weeks. By the time I was released, I had turned seventeen years old. Federal agents picked me up, and as I was leaving, one guard walked past and said, "Arrest that terrorist." I didn't give a damn what he said; I was so excited to be leaving. The whole world could burn down—as long as I was leaving, I didn't care.

CHAPTER 7

Changed

When I got back to New York, I was so excited and happy to be home again that I forgot I had to wear an ankle bracelet. I told myself everything was going to go back to normal, but I knew deep down that things would never be normal for me again. A lot of that feeling came from the fact that I was so traumatized by my experience. When I came back to my house, my mom had to sign papers and then they released me. They put the ankle bracelet on me the same day. The man who put the bracelet on me told me, "If you take it off, we're going to put you in jail. If your phone is off and we can't contact you, you're going to jail." That was the most effective threat anyone could ever make to me because I never wanted to be detained again. They never said how long I would have to wear the ankle bracelet; its removal was pending my immigration case.

Once a week I had to report to Federal Plaza so they could check the bracelet. The first time I went to one of these checkups,

I recognized that Federal Plaza was the building where my father and I had been taken for questioning. When I looked at it, my heart started pounding in my chest. It triggered horrible memories of the morning we were taken and of my time in the detention center, and I started to cry without any control. Seeing that building again was one of the most traumatizing moments of my life.

For days after my release, my mom didn't want to talk at all because she thought the government was recording us through the ankle bracelet. She would always shush me when I spoke. I'd say, "They're not listening." I didn't know if they were listening or not and I didn't care. I'd get on the phone with

Demaris, my friend from high school, and we would say bad things on purpose, things like, "We hate the government!"

Besides wearing the ankle bracelet and checking in every week, I was also under curfew, which at first was ten p.m. and then eleven p.m. Every night our phone would ring and I'd answer it, press a button on the ankle bracelet, and hang up. This would confirm I was home by my curfew All of this caused me so much stress that I couldn't sleep. I wore the ankle bracket for three years. I still have bruises from it to this day; my heel is black and always hurts.

My dad was deported in 2006. That was

the hardest part of all of it. I couldn't see him for a long time after I got released from the detention center. He was being held in New Jersey and I wasn't allowed to go visit him because it was outside of the range I could travel with my ankle bracelet. My mom and my siblings were able to visit, but they weren't able to go often because it cost a lot of money to get there. The government made an exception to let me travel to New Jersey just once, right before my dad was deported. I couldn't look at him. I just cried the entire time. He said, "I hope you take care of the family. It's your job." He was always concerned about taking care of the family, and as the oldest of my siblings, I had to take over his role. "It's your responsibility. You're the next person in line," he told me.

I miss a lot about my dad. I miss his company. I even miss him yelling at me. My siblings and I used to walk around saying our dad was strict, but we needed him. I miss him being the one who took care of everything. I didn't have to worry about everything when he was around. I didn't have to worry about bills or feeding my family.

I thought I was going to be able to go back to school, that the government was going to apologize and write me a check and I would be set for life, but it didn't go that way at all. When I came back to my life in New York, I had to drop out of school to work to support my family. There was no way my dad could work in Guinea; there are no jobs there. So I had to support my father, his family, my mom's family, and my family here, too. I worked three or four jobs at a time, whatever kind of job I could find, whether I was babysitting or cleaning houses. I worked at an interpretive service provider for a while until I found out that could get me sent back to jail because I didn't have any documentation. At times we were starving. For days there would be no food in the house. I started feeling distant from my friends because I was going through something that none of them could understand. I was growing up really quickly, maturing much faster than the people I had spent time with when I was younger. Finally, my family and I met a social worker who told us that we could get public assistance. Nobody had told us about the helpful stuff; it seemed like they wanted us to fail.

I didn't want my siblings to have to work at all. I didn't want them to miss out on what I missed out on, but I was drained. When I came back to New York, I was emotional. I would come home from work angry, like, *Leave me alone, don't touch me.* Now that I look back, I wish there was something that could have been done. I wish I would have told my story to a newspaper, but I was always afraid to say something, because I was always threatened with being sent to jail. That's why I kept so silent and cried about everything. My family wouldn't have been able to stand on their own feet without me. Everything that I do in life is to take care of my family. Everything in my life revolves around them.

CHAPTER 8

Freed

After a two-year immigration trial, I was finally granted asylum in 2007. During one of the immigration hearings, my mother got on the stand and testified about how she had been circumcised in Guinea, about the awful experience of it. I was granted asylum in the United States on the grounds that I would face forcible circumcision if I was deported to Guinea. The ankle bracelet had remained locked on me up until I got asylum. The day it was taken off, I couldn't stop smiling—a big, cheesy grin stayed on my face all day. I went to Federal Plaza, to the guy I had reported to every week, and when he took off the ankle bracelet, I said, "My legs! That's what my legs look like!" But for at least a year following its removal, I still felt like I had the ankle bracelet on. Sometimes I would be out late and I would think, Oh my God, my curfew, and start to panic. I can never fully relax and feel safe. Even though I am allowed to be in the United States, I am not American. I have asylum. That means I am a refugee.

In 2009, two years after I was granted asylum, I arranged to take a vacation to Texas with some friends. When I tried to board my flight at LaGuardia Airport, a ticket agent told me I was on the No Fly List. Federal agents came and handcuffed me. I thought back to when I was sixteen, to the early morning in my family's apartment when I was handcuffed for the first time. The agents took me to the airport security station, where I was held for almost thirteen hours in fear and confusion before I was released and went home.

A little while after that incident, I started working as a nanny for a nice family. I met them through an old friend who was also working for them. They spoiled me too much—beyond spoiled me. They paid me on time; they took care of me; they gave me Christmas bonuses; they gave me vacations; they took me everywhere with them. I was supposed to fly to Chicago with them for a family vacation in April 2010. I went to the airport before them because I was concerned about there being some kind of issue with me flying. I was at the airport with my luggage and I had brought a friend because I was afraid of experiencing what had happened the last time I tried to fly. I didn't know why, but I had a feeling that something was going to happen. I even called my lawyers beforehand, but they said that everything should be fine. But when I got to LaGuardia Airport, something did happen, the same issue as before. The airline supervisor called the Port Authority police and some other government officials. I called my one of my lawyers and he came. The police kept questioning me, asking, "What did you do to be on the No Fly List?"

In the end, I wasn't able to get on the plane. The family was disappointed and had to take their other babysitter. They were going to pay me for going on the trip with them. I lost money that day, money I was counting on and desperately needed. As soon as I got out of the airport interrogation room that day, something in me just triggered. I told myself, I'm done. I'm tired. I am not going to go through this again. I told my ACLU lawyers,

"I want to sue them," so we filed a lawsuit against Attorney General Eric Holder, FBI Director Robert Mueller, and Director of the Terrorist Screening Center Timothy Healy. They told my lawyers if I didn't go through with the lawsuit, they would take me off the No-Fly List. We made a verbal agreement. About a month later, we received a letter from James Kennedy of the Department of Homeland Security Traveler Redress Inquiry Program, but it didn't tell me why I wasn't allowed to board my flight at LaGuardia or what would happen if I tried to fly again.

In November 2010, a friend of mine gave me a ticket to fly to Chicago as a gift. I didn't know if I could fly, but I didn't know how to find out if I could without going to the airport and trying. Again, it was LaGuardia. I walked up to the ticket machine, punched in my name, and it told me I needed to see a ticket agent. I felt defeated; I just knew I wasn't going to be allowed to fly. I went to the counter and gave the ticket agent my name and my state ID. He printed the ticket.

I looked at him and said, "You printed it?"

He said, "Yeah."

"And it went through?"

"Yeah."

When he handed me my ticket, I started

to cry. He just stared at me, like, *Is this girl nuts?* I didn't care. I felt a little bit of freedom for the first time in a long while.

I grew up too fast. I experienced some things that a lot of people around me never have and never will, so it's hard to relate to my peers. Although the ankle bracelet is gone and I'm allowed to board planes, I've never really gotten to escape. All my friends went to college and graduated and I haven't even started yet. I certainly have a wider perspective on life because of my experiences, but I feel like things are not changing as quickly as I want them to. I want to be done with school; I want to have my own car; I want to be in my own space. I want to live my life. I don't mind taking care of my family, but for once, I want to do something for myself. I want to go and do something overseas. I want to be a traveling nurse. I want to help people. I want to educate.

Even though everything is said and done, I still live in constant fear of federal agents taking me or any of my family members. They disrupted my life when I was completely innocent and I'm well aware that they could do it again. I have so much to lose, including my family. I remember the look of helplessness on my mother's and siblings' faces the day they took me and my father away. Still, the United States is my home. It's the only place I really know. I am hopeful for this country because of people like me and my siblings. We know how it feels to suffer, so we have the motivation to change things.

Now I study Islam on my own. I still believe in God, because I feel like things could have been worse; I could have been deported and circumcised or I could have been sent to Guantánamo Bay. I still have my family. I still have my health. So, in a way, I know there is still God. There is always something to believe in at the end of the day.

Continue the Discussion

Was Adama's personal experience unusual?

Although Adama was one of the first women accused of terrorism, her detention and immigration case were not unusual. Less than two months after 9/11, the government had secretly detained at least a thousand individuals for criminal and immigration charges. Many advocacy groups believed these secret arrests to be unjust and racially motivated.

Did many Muslims in the United States experience physical and verbal harm after 9/11?

Yes, anti-Muslim sentiment was high, and many Muslims in the United States faced harassment and violence. Before 9/11, approximately 20 to 30 Muslim hate crimes were reported each year in the United States. In 2001, the reported number of Muslim hate crimes increased to almost 500. In 2018, the FBI reported 270 hate crimes against Muslims and Arab Americans.

Were many Muslim men, like Adama's father, detained and then deported?

After 9/11, thousands of immigrants were deported. In 2002, as part of the War on Terror the government created a program to register undocumented immigrant men from twenty-five countries that were predominately Muslim countries. Of the over eighty thousand men who volunteered to participate in the program, thirteen thousand were placed in deportation hearings, and none were charged as terrorists. Many individuals of Middle Eastern and South Asian descent felt fearful of the U.S. government, and advocacy groups considered the deportations to be unjust and racially motivated.

How did United States airport travel change after the 9/11 attacks and later attempted attacks?

Shortly after the 9/11 attacks, the government created a new federal agency, the Transportation Security Administration (TSA), to manage airport security; in 2003, TSA became part of the Department of Homeland Security. TSA introduced new airport security measures and now requires passengers to remove shoes, travel with a limited amount of liquids, and undergo full body scans and pat-downs. Additionally, only ticketed passengers are allowed at the airport gate. The government created the No Fly List, which the Terrorist Screening Center (TSC) maintains today.

What is Adama doing now?

In 2010, Adama fell in love and married a man, and her father was able to return to the United States on a U visa. The story of her experience was featured in *Patriot Acts*, a book about post-9/11 injustices, and *Adama*, a short documentary film. As part of the film's release, she spoke to audiences about her arrest, imprisonment, and mistreatment by the American government.

Adama believes she can be of service to others because of experience, and she is working on starting a nonprofit. She remains close to her family and spends as much time as she can with them. Adama lives in New York.

Timeline

2000

Adama attends an Islamic boarding school in Buffalo, New York.

2001

September 11: Two planes crash into the Twin Towers of the World Trade Center in New York City, a third plane hits the Pentagon near Washington, D.C., and a fourth crashes in a field in Pennsylvania. Almost three thousand people are killed as a result of these terrorist attacks, carried out by Islamic extremists.

September 17: Reports of hate crimes against Muslims begin to rise.

November 5: The Justice Department announces over a thousand people have been secretly detained for criminal and immigration charges. Many of those held in custody are Middle Eastern men.

October 26: Congress passes the Patriot Act, which increases government surveillance powers and is meant to prevent terrorist attacks.

November: On her way to New York City, Adama experiences verbal harassment and extra security screenings at the airport.

December 22: A British citizen hides explosives in his shoes and tries to blow up an airplane. He is arrested for the attempted terrorist attack.

2002

Adama returns to public school in New York City.

November 25: President Bush signs the Homeland Security Act, creating the Department of Homeland Security.

2003

The FBI creates the Terrorist Screening Center to identify known or suspected terrorists, and a group of individuals in their database are placed on the No Fly List.

2005

March 24: Officials forcibly enter Adama's home, and Adama and her father are detained.

May 9: Adama is released from a juvenile detention center in New Jersey and begins to wear an electronic ankle monitor.

2006

March 9: President Bush signs the Patriot and Terrorism Reauthorization Act, permitting the Patriot Act to continue.

August: Adama's father is deported; soon after, Adama drops out of high school to support her family.

2007

September 27: After a two-year immigration trial, Adama is granted political asylum, which allows her to stay in the United States. She is able to remove the electronic ankle monitor.

2009

Adama attempts to board a plane at LaGuardia Airport and is not allowed to fly.

2010

Adama's father returns to the United States on a U visa.

April 13: Once again, Adama attempts to board a plane at LaGuardia Airport and is not allowed to fly.

June 30: The ACLU files a lawsuit against the U.S. government challenging the No Fly List, and Adama is one of several plaintiffs.

November 11: Adama is able to board her flight at LaGuardia Airport.

Acknowledgments

Thank you to my parents Mamadou and Aissatou and to my siblings Alpha, Maraima, Abdoul, and Saeed. They endured so much, stayed by my side, and supported me no matter what.

Thank you, David, my teacher, my friend, and my brother. When I was so afraid to speak, he gave me a voice, stood by me, and supported me no matter what!

Thank you, John Wilkinson, a public advocate who became a brother and who supported my family and me in many ways.

Finally, thank you to Deleen Carr and Iris Mencia, the two women who I consider my moms.

About I, Witness

I, Witness is a nonfiction book series that tells important stories of real young people who have faced and conquered extraordinary contemporary challenges. There's no better way for young readers to learn about the world's issues and upheavals than through the eyes of young people who have lived through these times.

Proceeds from this book series support the work of the International Alliance of Youth Writing Centers and its sixty-plus member organizations. These nonprofit writing centers are joined in a common belief that young people need places where they can write and be heard, where they can have their voices celebrated and amplified.

www.youthwriting.org